I0839852

THE EMBODIMENT

OF ABOLITION

Jeff Hood

Alli Sullivan

Foreword, Anthony Sanchez

Afterword, Mike Zoosman

Cover, Hannah

For the Executed.

CONTENTS,

I. Foreword, Anthony Sanchez

II. Humanity

III. The Fight

IV. Rage

V. Grief

VI. Truth

VII. Isolation

VIII. Success

IX. "The Fight for Anthony Sanchez": Last Minute Reflections on the Death of God and an Innocent Man,

X. "I died standing for my innocence rather than begging for clemency on my knees"

XI. Afterword, Mike Zoosman

FOREWORD,

This is not the way I expected it to end. I guess we all

hope for a different conclusion. For most of us, this path

that I'm taking is the one that most of us will take.

Regardless, I want to encourage you to think for yourself.

You don't need a bunch of advocates and lawyers telling

you what is right or wrong for you. If you want to do

clemency, do that shit. If you don't want to do clemency,

fuck it. Make the right decision for you. Nobody else.

You. Also, I realize that my case has caused a bunch of

drama. While that wasn't my intention, I'm not sad

about it. The more attention that is on all of our cases the

better. With regards to advocates and lawyers, trust what

they do not what they say. Remember, talk is cheap.

Anybody can send out a bunch of shit and stir the pot.

Few can actually get our cases out there and get shit

done.

Anthony Sanchez

September 20, 2023

Executed, September 21, 2023

HUMANITY,

Our work is about making humanity humane. It is important to note that humanity is not intrinsically humane. In fact, it seems to be the exact opposite. There is so much evil everywhere. Then again, the humane comes from the human. So, there must be some good left somewhere.

We encounter the self in the other. The humane connection comes from the human connection. Letters. Cards. Visits. Phone calls. These are the things that create the human connection…and in the human connection we find the humane. We learn to advocate based on the relationships that we foster with those we are advocating for.

Everybody wants to call these guys monsters. Perhaps the monster in them is the monster in us? We're not all that different…we just are…monsters.

More specifically, we come to a fullness of comprehension when we allow our thoughts to reside on death row. If we can imagine ourselves there, we can begin to imagine the humanity that resides there.

Dehumanization is a trap. We think it is a normal phenomenon. Slowly, we become a part of the dehumanization. Then…before we know it…we too have been dehumanized. When we fight for these folks on death row, we fight for our own humanity. Death row is a place of death because we have made it so. If we are to bring life to such a space, we must bring our humanity to the table.

Light is created by the spark that exists between you and the other; that ultimately makes the other no longer the other. True human interaction is a symphony of light. The relationships fostered on death row create light…without them…there is none.

There is darkness amongst us. It resides in the hearts of those who are so comfortable killing. The people who work at these facilities are light blockers. It is our job to bring the light in. To demand human relationship. To demand hope. To be light.

One of the things that we regularly do is record various conversations with the folks that we work with. Their voices give evidence of humanity. Their voices remind us of our responsibility to be humane.

Truthfully, these folks are just like anyone else. Some are kind. Some are generous. Some are assholes. Some are innocent. Some are guilty. Some are somewhere in between. Ultimately…. They're not God. They're not the devil. They're not angels. They're not demons. They're not perfect. They're human. They're us.

Deep empathy accompanies deep humanity. We must bring the fullness of ourselves to the struggle. Don't hold back. There is no fear in love. To deny the self is to deny humanity…not to embrace it.

We must see death rows as places where humans reside. Nothing more. Nothing less. Existence is the beginning of empathy. It doesn't matter what the human has done…the human is human.

Hate is not humane. The way we treat our enemies says much about our humanity. So many find it easier to love the people on death row than those who want the people on death row executed. We must fight the temptation of hate. That is the only way that we can love.

Humans do not vanish. We exist in each other and with each other. You are. They are. We are.

One must see in order to be seen. It is our job to show both the self and the other.

Connection is intrinsic to the abolitionist experience. We create humanity to humanize all parties involved…including that which is within.

The FIGHT,

What does it mean to fight for the individuals on death row? To fight as an abolitionist? From our experiences, if you want to get into this work, you need to have a really strong backbone. This work is not for the faint of heart. In a line of work with very few wins, where the stakes are incredibly high, you need to have some fight in you. You need to have the fight in you to keep going; to keep on struggling. And when you get knocked down, you need to have the fight to get back up.

Underlying this fight is a sort of moral understanding that the death penalty is just inherently wrong, and that we are fighting against this massive evil. There can be nothing good with the death penalty. But there is something more to this work than just secular discomfort. There is discomfort in the soul, and when you function from the soul, you can keep up the fight far longer than when you're simply functioning from an intellectual place. Many of us have gotten our 30-second elevator pitches down, citing the many rational reasons that the death penalty is wrong, delivering them to anyone who will listen; whether we're at the Fast and Vigil in front of the US Supreme Court, in the airport, or at the grocery store. It's one thing to recite a whole slew of statistics and figures, but no matter how many facts you lay on someone, without the personal experience; without knowing someone who has gone through execution; without going through it yourself; without engaging with the issue on a person level: your fight just does not have the same vigor.

We think that in this line of work, having direct relationships with various individuals on death row is so important, because it creates that soul connection to the issue. We've seen some people in the movement – they don't make those relationships. We get it. Forming strong relationships with real people who are condemned to die only magnifies the trauma, the "hits" we experience on a daily basis. It feels radically different to form these relationships on death row only to see these individuals murdered at the hands of the state one after the next. But without those connections, those relationships, those friendships, just seeing those people as human beings, it's extremely difficult to keep up the motivation to fight for them in the way that you would have if you had gotten to know them on a personal level.

Certainly someone who is not aligned with death penalty abolition does not have a fight in them. However, there are many people – a majority of Americans – who fundamentally oppose executions, without a very personal connection to the struggle, lack the motivation to go beyond simply saying they're against capital punishment.

We oppose executions in general, but it absolutely feels different when you don't know the individual, they're not someone you're closely connected with. For us, one cannot be a true abolitionist without at least some level of real, human engagement with the folks on the rows. To keep the struggle pounding on, you need to have the fight in you, and how can you have the fight if you don't have something or someone that you're fighting for?

Those who have a personal connection to the work really define and differentiate those who are "full-on" abolitionists and those who simply just oppose it. We live in a space where we have to think about the struggle against the death penalty as being a bottom-up, not a top-down, issue, meaning the only way to bring folks who are on death row to the table in their own right, to fight for their own cause, is to form meaningful relationships with them. To be a true abolitionist is to empower the folks we fight for; folks who have been disempowered for far too long by a system that is out for vengeance.

As abolitionists, when we think about "the fight," we think about going to the legislature and speaking at rallies, but the real fight is to remind these folks on death row of their own humanity. Often we become distracted in this work and are fighting to just keep the person physically alive, but we cannot forget that the fight is just as much about helping these individuals remain emotionally and spiritually alive. It's difficult for these folks on the row to remain emotionally and spiritually alive when one after the other, they witness individuals they have come to know and love as family be hauled off, likely never to return, knowing they may be next.

In many ways, this fight is not just a fight, but a war. It is literally a fight to the death. We are exhausting absolutely every resource we can find to make sure that does not happen, but we are up against a state that has an arsenal of resources infinitely greater than ours, dead set on making sure we don't win. There is a powerful song that comes to mind in this discussion called "Let Me Hurt" by Emily Rowed, in which she describes being in a war "with no armor." Alli found herself listening to it constantly around Arthur Brown Jr.'s execution, not only because his execution filled us with such immense rage, but because it can often feel like no matter what we do, we are losing. It's incredibly easy to spiral down to a pit of hopelessness and despair, where it does not feel like we will ever win.

But we must remember, especially if we forge relationships in this work, that we must be prepared to get hurt. Part of being in the struggle is being able to take the knocks and keep going; to have that fuel, and that spiritual energy that comes from believing in what you're doing.

We talk about having to get up and keep going, but that does not mean we don't experience burnout and fatigue. In fact, it's something that we experience often because of how draining this work can be. The fuel to keep going comes not only from the personal relationships but the loss of those relationships when people you care about are killed. We wish there was a way that we could stay motivated and energized in this work without there being so much grief. Working to abolish the death penalty and stop executions comes with such a rollercoaster of emotions, between all the last minute legal filings, winning in one court only for another to throw the issue out, but still clinging onto hope that something will give. There is always hope until it is over. This is arguably the most exhausting part of the work.

RAGE,

Arthur Brown died less than 24 hours ago. We have been forever changed, our souls filled with rage, and our hearts with despair. Not only did Arthur's family lose their loved one, but the Harris County prosecutor's office knowingly lied and manipulated the victim's families and the entire city of Houston for more than three decades into believing Arthur was this cold-blooded monster. To worsen everything, it is almost certain that when the State of Texas executed Arthur's co-defendant, Marion Dudley in 2006, they executed another innocent man.

Arthur Brown Jr. was the 583rd person executed by the state of Texas since they resumed executions in 1982 following the Gregg decision.

"What is occurring here tonight is not justice, it's murder of an innocent man for a murder that occurred in 1992. For the last 30 years I've proven my innocence to the courts, but the courts blocked me and then refused me access to the ballistics for 20 years; I've proven facts and ballistics to be false. It's been 30 years now, the state refused to turn over evidence. Nine of the ten trial motions were filed for discovery of evidence, but each were denied each time. I asked for DNA, I was denied DNA. My co-defendant was executed in 2006 and if I'm innocent he was innocent and they killed an innocent man, and the state doesn't want the truth to come out.

They won't allow me DNA. The victim's son identified on audio tape it wasn't me or the co-defendant. The state hid the evidence so long and good that my own attorneys couldn't find it. Tonight, Texas will kill a second innocent man for a murder that occurred in 1992. I have no further words."

There is a tendency to see rage as evil. Such a tendency is not just problematic but completely contrary to the pursuit of justice. One cannot fight for justice unless they are enraged by injustice.

Life then murder. There are not enough words to describe what this feeling is like. It is such an unnatural, abnormal, bizarre feeling. Yes it's grief, but it's grief in a way that so few people ever experience. Grief is a very normal part of the human condition, but experiencing grief, following the murder of somebody – and not just the murder of somebody, but the intentional, premeditated murder of somebody that was planned for and that you were waiting for and you were counting down the days and hours and minutes for – is just so bizarre. Rage is a beyond appropriate reaction.

Whether you know them or not…. Overwhelmed. Heartbroken. Devastated. Such feelings lead to a rage that keeps the fight alive. It's a fuel. Intimacy seems to make the fire burn faster, stronger and brighter. There is a piece of you burning…burning with rage. The soul is made to feel such things. To burn but not burn out.

Arthur Brown doesn't rest in peace. On the contrary, Brown was murdered and his soul will never rest in peace until these unnecessary killings stop. We shouldn't enjoy any sort of peace either. These executions should *haunt* us day in and day out. The disturbance should never let us rest. In our ears, may we hear their names. Over and over, Arthur Brown…Arthur Brown…Arthur Brown.

Rise up in power. Rage for justice. Rest when it stops.

There are no stages to a grief like this. You can't go through stages because the grief doesn't stop. The grief simply is. Hope seems to be executed and reborn with every execution. Life dies. Life lives.

Without a doubt, people don't see these executions like we do. If they did, they would stop. Most just live blissfully ignorant. Blissfully unaware that they are murderers. Such numbness sucks the soul out of our society. Such numbness must be counteracted by rage. It is our job to demand that society see.

Watching people die doesn't get easier. With each last breath, it becomes harder and harder to breathe. Rage becomes the oxygen that keeps the fight alive.

Fight. Don't stop. Fight.

Grief is a luxury for those not facing the next execution. It's as if you spend too much time grieving the last execution, you will fail to be present for the next. There are so many more in line. We can't stop. In the midst of such horror, it seems like rage is the only feeling worth feeling.

Perhaps, there is a balance. You want to honor the person who has been executed. You don't want an execution to overshadow the majesty of who they were…who they still are. But you must rage. There is no way to honor their memory without rage. It's an incredibly complicated juxtaposition. Then again, maybe it's not…maybe it is just about rage. Honor is rage and rage is honor.

There is no meaning in an execution. It is senseless. There is meaning in resistance. We are the meaning. We are the rage.

Stop trying to make sense of it all. Simply feel. Rage.

It is bizarre to fan the flames of rage. We are told not to feel such things. Those of us who are called to live through it all know that such feelings are inescapable and should be fostered…until our rage burns the death penalty to the ground, once and for all.

GRIEF,

How do you remain human amid constant death? You must allow room for grief. You can't give quarter to numbness. Such numbness is suicide. You will cease to exist. You must feel it deep in your soul.

Grieve for the victims. Grieve for the participants. Grieve for the condemned. Grieve for the government. Grieve.

We are amid a moral apocalypse. Grieve.

People are happy about the execution. Grieve.

I don't know what to say. Grieve.

They see us as the enemy. Grieve.

There is so much hate. Grieve.

Where do we go from here? Grieve.

Surely, grief must be both an origination and a
destination for the abolitionist.

TRUTH,

Integrity. The first thing we think about when it comes to truth– that ultimately, we don't get into this work to make shit up. Contrary to what many who don't agree with us believe, we get into this work to promote truth… that truth is sometimes difficult.

The truth is often that the person we are working with has done a horrible, horrible thing, but that ultimately they still do not deserve to be executed. Other times, the truth is that the person we are working with is innocent and does not deserve to pay for something someone else did.

The truth remains that capital punishment is morally problematic under any circumstance. For us, maintaining our integrity is among the most important things to maintain in the midst of all of this. We feel that not all activists prioritize integrity, which is why people sometimes think that activists are crazy as hell. And they're not always wrong.

We must be willing to recognize that not everyone is innocent. In fact, only a small percentage of these individuals condemned to die are innocent, but it's still high enough to be an immense locus of concern. For us to be set free from capital punishment, we must be willing to tell the truth, the truth that the death penalty is wrong, but also the truth about these cases. It can be really difficult. We want to go in believing everyone; or at least that those who say they are innocent, are

innocent.

What would you expect of someone who says that

they're innocent? When we go into new situations and

meet new individuals who are condemned to die, we tend

to be really skeptical. We've met individuals who have

said they were innocent, but it does not really add up, or

the person you meet is not someone who you align with.

Often once we go in and get to know the individual, our

experiences with them can pretty quickly skew our

perceptions of them one way or the other, even before we

see the evidence. After we first met Arthur Brown Jr.,

despite coming from a very skeptical place, we were

inclined to believe in his innocence claim because we had

an incredibly difficult time believing that someone who

cared so much about other people's wellbeing could have committed the horrible thing Texas alleges he committed.

We did not want to lose credibility and it took us until the last couple of weeks to begin asserting Arthur's innocence to ensure that the information we were putting out there was truthful. With Arthur, because truth is so important to us, it bit us in the ass. Arthur had been screaming this truth for 30 years and we only listened in the last few weeks when there was tangible proof. People are very skeptical of activist's positions on things, especially with death penalty cases, because the vast majority of Americans are led to believe that the system we have is foolproof.

That's simply not true. The system is not truthful. If the system were truthful, the public would be less likely to blindly support it like they do now.

Cameroonian political theorist and anthropological scholar, Achille Mbembe, argues that the "ultimate expression of sovereignty resides" in the state's "power and capacity to dictate who may live and who must die." Such a concept, he argues, is rooted in modernity, specifically the "colonial world." To Mbembe, the existence of "the Other" is central to creating a "fictionalized notion of the enemy;" an exaggerated threat to "life and security" that necessitates the killing of them. By exaggerating the necessity to kill certain people, in this case folks on death row, states are able to "'civilize'" the ways of killing and "attribute rational objectives to them," thereby co-opting the public into supporting the killing efforts rather than challenging them.

When someone is sent to death row, or even just prison, for a serious crime they are immediately banished to the status of "the Other". The government and media strip them of their holistic identity turning them into "monsters" in the eyes of the public, whether each individual actually did what they are accused of or not. It's a perfect recipe for exaggerating the threat to "life and security", whereby the state can justify the "necessity" to kill them.

The *State of Exception,* a leading tenant of Mbembe's worldview, is when there is a "temporal suspension of the state of law." However, I would take it a step further and suggest that it may not only be a "suspension" of the state of law, but also a suspension of all that is moral and acceptable in a given society. For Mbembe, the dangers of *power* rest in the state's abilities to manipulate the public into supporting unnecessary violence where they otherwise would not tolerate it.

Ask any person in the United States whether they believe killing another person was acceptable. Without any additional conditions, I can guarantee you almost all of them would be disturbed by the question and agree that it is never acceptable to kill another person. However, when that person is someone who has been completely demonized by the state, who is convicted of an absolutely heinous crime, who the government continues to manipulate the public into believing is a "monster", we find ourselves in a *State of Exception* in the United States. The only reason Americans are tolerating these kinds of abuses of power is because they have been co-opted into believing that there is a "rational objective" to kill people who have been condemned by the state.

The vast majority of pro "tough on crime" folks are simultaneously in favor of small government because they don't trust the government to act in the best interest of its citizens. However, when it comes to the government extending its reach of power to pick and choose who dies, those same folks seem to conveniently forget that such an expression of power is not conducive with small government. A *State of Exception* inconspicuously forces society to abandon all of its moral standards, becoming complacent in egregious acts of violence they wouldn't ordinarily support.

No one is winning when our government can decide who they want to kill. Not the folks on death row and certainly not the United States of America. Such a condition disempowers everyone in our country who is not actively fighting against such violence from resisting the abuses of the state. The state doesn't care about any one of us, just like it does not care about the individuals who are condemned to die; it's merely using us to do its dirty work and we don't even have a clue.

Ultimately, is the goal truth, or is it to save a life? That answer differs between who you ask. We think almost every death penalty abolitionist will say the goal is to save a life, and some people will put that above truth. If we genuinely believe that the person we are working with is telling the truth based on their character and the person we have gotten to know, we will gladly spread the truth. But for a lot of activists and death penalty abolitionists, saving a life is more important. It's a weird, and often uncomfortable place to be in, because of course we want to save everyone's life– that's why we do this work, because we don't think any person should be executed regardless of what they did or did not do. But, maintaining our own integrity as an organization, as individual activists, and as people is vital because it will not help our movement if we are out here shouting things that are not true. Perhaps it may help that one person in the moment, but it is not in the best interest of the movement in general.

It's difficult. We are focused on what could do the greatest good for the greatest amount of people, but we were recently asked if we would lie to save a life. We don't know that it's necessarily the right answer but we think our answer would be yes. It just shows how broken, and evil, and malicious the system that we are up against is – that we might have to lie to save a life.

Everyone should be concerned with the truth and it is really unfortunate that we might have to put saving a life above truth because we should not have to do that. But in the battle we are in, we are sometimes forced to do that. It forces us to consider if we are situational ethicists or virtue ethicists, and we think our response would be that we are virtue ethicists. We must tell the truth even if it's not comfortable.

We have to tell the truth in order to be truth and in order to be right. We can't do right without being right. It's a strange place to be in.

Does this movement matter more than the person?

It's a very difficult question to answer because on one hand our goal is to save individual people, however, as abolitionists, our objective is to stop the whole system so that nobody has to go through this torturous process. As we continue to work towards the end goal, we cannot just forget about individual people along the way, which our movement sometimes does. Our movement is often more focused on where we're headed instead of being present and addressing things as they come. There must be a place for both. We can't lose track of where we're at because we are so focused on where we're going.

The goal is truth. And abolition is truth– so the goal is abolition. Each case, taken at its best, can lead us in that direction.

ALONE,

This work is a work of solitude. You can't be an abolitionist if you can't stand alone. People love killing too much. Most of the time nobody is going to want to stand with you.

I made contact. I wrote letters. I went to prison. I visited. I watched him die. I was alone.

I got arrested. I was put in jail. I went to court. I was on probation. I was alone.

I walked in protest. I dodged cars. I stood my ground. I was threatened. I was alone.

Being alone is part of the gig.

The people that you love are most often going to be killed.

This is a unique place to be.

Knowing that your work will most likely leave you alone.

Isolation was all that I experienced after my friend was executed.

Isolation was all that I experienced after my friend was executed.

It's so common that we both said it simultaneously.

What more can one do than give all that they have? Yet, when you give all that you have, you end up alone. The abolitionist does it over and over. The cycle never seems to end.

You don't even have to have known them to feel their loss. In knowing the rejection and isolation, you know them.

Bizarre. That's the only way to describe this solitude.

We've never heard of grief counseling for abolitionists.

Maybe we should have.

This is not the type of movement that puts thousands of

people in the streets. It's just us. Yet, we know of no

other movement that such small numbers have such a big

impact. You can stand alone and change the world.

Isolation almost becomes the vehicle for change.

SUCCESS,

Success comes in many different forms when we're talking about the death penalty; abolition work. Certainly stopping someone's execution or exonerating someone or getting them off of death row are all extremely big successes. However, in this work, we take so many hits that it's really important for us to find success everywhere, even when they are small successes along the way.

With Arthur Brown Jr, we didn't stop his execution, but we were able to spread the truth about his case. The truth is that he did not commit the horrifying crime he was accused of. People learned the truth about his case. We planted seeds of doubt into the minds of the public. We made it so that Arthur was not alone in the final moments of his life.

Success can mean many things in our work. Success has to do with humanity. We fight for people's humanity, not just their physical humanity. We're not just talking about saving lives. We're talking about saving spirits– helping people to understand who they are. That they matter. That their families matter. That the families of the victims matter. To show our society that these people matter and that they are not disposable.

The families of the victims and those executed are the forgotten ones. They receive just as much backlash as the person being executed, as if they are responsible for the individual going to death row. It's important that we show up not just for the person being executed but for all of the families. Not just painting the humanity of the person being executed for themselves but for their families too. These families carry the reputations of their loved ones that will stick with them forever.

The victim's families find a certain level of humanity. It's easy for them to think that if we can get the person who killed their loved one executed then their lives will all of a sudden be better. And we know that it is not true. Everytime someone is executed, we are ALL worse off. This conversation is broader than just, "let's execute the monster." That's not to say that many of these people have not done horrible, horrible things. When you smash your kid's head in, that's pretty horrible. Beating people to death and killing a baby are monstrosities. But what these folks on death row show is that the monster in me is the monster in you. That ultimately we all have darkness in us. And part of what we feel in our work is about helping people, and helping the general public to realize we are not all that far removed from the people on death row.

Often we kill these guys with the idea that if we kill them, we are getting rid of our own sin, our own monstrosity, our own evil. Success is to help the people sitting at home look at the person being executed and see themselves in that person. Success can look many different ways in this work.

If we impact anybody, whether they're on our side, whether they're not on our side, whether they're undecided, whether they're party to this process by choice or not, anytime we can impact them on any level that is not just beneficial to our cause, but society at large is success. Impacting any of these people that think the death penalty is a good thing, the people that think we need the death penalty to attain "justice", and think that the only way we can move on is if we kill these monsters. It's a success to be able to impact them in any way, in any tiny amount, to see that this is not the only way we can live or should live, especially because we aren't going to dismantle the death penalty overnight. It's our job to always remind people that there's a way out of the killing cycle; there is a turnoff before.

It does not have to be like this.

"The Fight for Anthony Sanchez": Last Minute Reflections on the Death of God and an Innocent Man,

"IS GOD DEAD?" Yes. I've seen it. For over a decade, I've worked with those whom our society has chosen to execute. I believe that God inhabits the least of these. I believe that God has died repeatedly…and we are the culprits of such a moral catastrophe. It takes courage to allow the mind and heart to journey to such a disturbing place. How can a dead God be worth believing in? On the contrary, perhaps a dead God is the only God worth believing in. Like the woman who reached out for the garment of God and was healed, sometimes it takes weaving through clarity to find something worth grasping for.

Dead Gods are strange teachers. The lessons they teach are not always clear. But like the woman found out, healing doesn't usually come from the clarity of rational behavior. You see, only the courageous get to be healed. The ones who choose to touch the dead.

Courage is an interesting cultural phenomenon. It's sort of a linguistical mirage. Everybody talks about it…but nobody seems to actually know the fullness of what they're describing. It is partial devoid of perfect. I've known partial. Then, I was surprised by the perfect.

Jesus the very incarnation of God is drowning in a world of fear and sorrow. Knowing that society is determined to kill him, Jesus asks those that he trusts to sit and watch with him…to engage what is to come…to be present…deadly present.

Sexual assault and murder are obviously not phenomenon one should look past. When I met Anthony Sanchez, I assumed that I was meeting someone who had sexually

assaulted and murdered a beautiful young woman named

Juli Busken. Even though Sanchez passionately claimed

otherwise, I assumed that he was full of shit. He

certainly wouldn't have been the first guy on death row

I'd met who was. I was wrong. Time has revealed new

truths. If we open our hearts, new truths can reveal to us

the fullness of God.

I investigated for myself. I read the transcripts. I

engaged the witnesses. I sought out experts. Slowly, I

came to a surprising conclusion…there was an innocent

man on death row in Oklahoma. Injustice was

metastasizing by the day. I knew that it was my duty to

sit and watch with him…to stand guard against an approaching moral catastrophe.

In Gethsemane, Jesus knew that he was the victim of a society determined to extract blood from an innocent man. Throughout human history, people seem determined to destroy that which is righteous and just. Instead of fleeing, Jesus remained in the Garden. On his knees, Jesus prays in anguish, "Is there any other way?" The forces of evil were at the gate.

From the beginning, Anthony Sanchez has known that his execution is more than possible. When people on death row find their backs against the wall, most are willing to say or do whatever it takes to save their life.

I've seen it…repeatedly. Sanchez is different. From the

beginning, he told me that he was not going to

compromise his claims of innocence under any

circumstance. He hasn't.

Consistently, Sanchez has hated his attorneys.

Repeatedly, they've proven unwilling or incapable of

fighting for his innocence, even going for almost six

years without communicating with him at one point. One

of the cruel twists of fate in our system is that justice is

something to be bought and if you don't have the means

then you are stuck with the attorneys you have. Such

legal hopelessness never deterred Sanchez from

maintaining that he was an innocent man.

When the possibility of execution came up, Sanchez told me that he would rather die than waiver in his declaration of innocence. I believe him. Surely, no life is not worth living if you lose your soul in the process. The more that I heard the more that I realized what my job was…remain steadfast in supporting Sanchez in his convictions while doing all that I can to save his life.

Jesus offered no physical resistance. He simply questioned the process, proclaimed his innocence and demanded justice. Injustice has a way of creating insurmountable processes amid assumptions or assignments of guilt. Unquestionably, Oklahoma is one of the epicenters of injustice.

In recent months, Anthony Sanchez has shown unbelievable courage. When he realized that the clemency process would involve an extrajudicial process that declared him to be a monster, his own attorneys refusal to advocate wholeheartedly for his innocence and his participation in a process insurmountably stacked against him, Sanchez decided to reject the opportunity. Even if it meant that he was giving up an opportunity to beg for his life, Sanchez was going to stick with his convictions. Repeatedly he has declared, "1 will not participate in a hearing that demands that I act guilty."

Unable to comprehend the inaction of his attorneys in any other way, Sanchez came to the belief that they wanted him to be executed. Even if that isn't true, there seems to be little doubt that all trust was gone. Instead of simply rolling over and taking their neglect, Sanchez made the decision to fire them, even if that meant acting as his own attorney in the final months of his life. Repeatedly he has declared, "I refuse to stand with anyone who will not stand with me." It is important to note that Sanchez is not dense to what his decisions could mean. The possibility of his execution looms large over every decision he makes. However, that's not his primary concern. Repeatedly, Sanchez has declared, "I would rather die standing on my feet in the knowledge of my innocence than begging on my knees for something that I didn't do."

Jesus knew what was likely. Unwaveringly, Jesus refused to move or even beg for his life. His convictions mattered much more to him than his life.

The parallels between Jesus' Gethsemane moment to Sanchez's current moment are too stark to be ignored. No matter what the cost, Jesus stuck by his principles, even to his detriment. Presently, the decisions that Sanchez has made are based on his principles, even to his possible detriment. Sanchez is an innocent man who refuses to act like a guilty one. He demands justice and justice alone. Sometimes, courage is not a mirage.

In those final hours, the disciples were told to watch and pray. Anthony Sanchez is asking the same of you. Do not fall asleep. Stay awake with us.

God doesn't have to die.

"I died standing for my innocence rather than begging for clemency on my knees.",

Anyone who knew Anthony Sanchez will tell you that he was the epitome of courage. He went to his death *"standing for [his] innocence rather than begging for clemency on [his] knees"*. He never once waivered from this — from the moment he was found guilty of Juli

Busken's murder in 2006 and uttered to her family, *"I swear to God, I didn't kill your daughter"*, through to his very last breath.

There were many individuals that had the power to intervene to stop this man-made horror and made a conscious decision not to. Judge Joe Heaton. Attorney General Gentner Drummond. Governor Kevin Stitt. Attorneys Mark Barrett and Randy Coyne. The US Supreme Court. The silence from our own movement as Oklahoma proceeded in killing this innocent man was disturbing. Everywhere we turned, it felt like we were being challenged not only by the state, but by folks in our own movement who are supposed to help us stop these executions.

Anthony and I spent all night "texting" and continued to do so right up until the moment they took him from the cell adjacent to the execution chamber to strap him down and get the IVs ready. He could not sleep. His mind was racing. He would forget what he wanted to say because he said his mind was just *"blank"*. I told him that it was "ok". Very few people go through the psychological torture of being executed — it was entirely appropriate if he couldn't calm his mind down.

In those final hours he told me over and over, *"this isnt right alli . i pinky swear i am innocent ... alli i pinky swear i am innocent how is this happening ?"*and one of the final things he told me was, *"what ever you do dont give up being a lawyer !"* Last August, when my dear friend, Kosoul Chanthakoummane, was being executed he said exactly the same thing to me. Both of these men had been wholly abandoned by the few people that are actually supposed to be on their side — their attorneys. At 4:16am CT Anthony reiterated his sentiments about his former attorneys, *"i dont understand how mark and randell can get away with what ther saying and doing to jeff an death penalty action an me"*.

Just a few days before Anthony's execution, Randy, Anthony's former attorney, suggested to the Associated Press that we were using the "myth of Anthony Sanchez, an innocent man facing his death, as a publicity fundraising campaign". Randy could not have been more wrong. We pushed Anthony's innocence so hard because his own attorneys refused to — we believed wholeheartedly that Anthony did not murder Juli Busken that cold December morning in 1996. Anthony's voice and agency were silenced for far too long. That needed to change.

Despite being in this work for some time and seeing just how few wins there are, I don't think any of us truly believed that it would have come down to this. Even in the final hours of Anthony's life, he kept asking me if I believed he still had a chance. We were waiting on SCOTUS to rule. Once something gets to SCOTUS, we are almost certain how it will end — even still, we had a chance. A small chance, but it was a chance — a chance, that something would give and Anthony would get some, any, amount of relief. I told him to hold onto that chance. It was all we had at that point.

We did not succeed in saving a life this time, but we succeeded in giving Anthony his voice. Many people along the way questioned Anthony's decisions, and suggested that he was being coerced by his spiritual advisor, but those of us who knew Anthony, know he made those decisions on his own. Anthony was courage. If he was going to do things, he was going to do them his way — and he did. In one of the final conversations he had with his spiritual advisor, Anthony affirmed that he had no regrets with how his campaign played out — *"If I had it to do all over again, I wouldn't change anything. I made the decisions that I had to make. With your help, I was able to be something more than a prisoner...a real person. Thank you, Jeff."*

We get into this work to make those on the inside feel seen — to make them human again. For far too long, condemned individuals have been stripped of their human-ness and made out to be something they are not. Anthony was no monster. He was no murderer. He was a son. A brother. A father. A grandfather. An artist. And he was our friend. Those of us who knew Anthony will tell you how much of a privilege it was to have known him. And how much of a void was left when his life was taken.

There is no justice in killing another person. And there certainly was no justice, yesterday, when Oklahoma murdered Anthony for something he did not do. Our world is not a better place without Anthony in it.

"Anthony Sanchez died how he lived, courageously standing upon his convictions rather than begging for mercy on his knees. May we all go and do likewise."
~The Rev. Dr. Jeff Hood

Rest in Power, dear friend. You are free, at last.

#FreeAnthonySanchez

AFTERWORD,

May this sacred testimony of Alli Sullivan and the Rev. Dr. Jeff Hood help to open hearts and minds to bring to fruition the *success* that these dyed-in-the-wool death penalty abolitionists envision. Every individual whose mind is changed on this issue, as mine was years ago, brings our society and humanity closer to victory in the mission - now more urgent than ever - of upholding the sanctity of life itself. The direct connections that Ms. Sullivan and Rev. Hood have forged with those facing imminent execution calls to mind the charge that Jewish philosopher Martin Buber made a century ago in his renowned volume *I and Thou*: "Spirit is not in the I but between I and You." It is that *Ruakh HaKodesh* - Holy Spirit - that drives the souls of so many abolitionists. It is no wonder that Buber joined many other Jewish human rights icons in his opposition to Israel's execution of Nazi war criminal Adolph Eichmann, which he called "a great mistake."

By bearing direct witness to human beings counting down their days to state-sponsored murder, Ms. Sullivan and Rev. Hood have born witness to the inherent psychological torture that occurs every single time the government puts to death a prisoner - innocent or guilty - against his or her will. It is for this reason that Albert Camus, in his *Reflections on the Guillotine (1957),* rightfully condemned any nation that puts its prisoners to death, writing:

> "But what then is capital punishment but the most premeditated of murders, to which no criminal's deed, however calculated it may be, can be compared? For there to be equivalence, the death penalty would have to punish a criminal who had warned his victim of the date at which he would inflict a horrible death on him and who, from that moment onward, had confined him at his mercy for months. Such a monster is not encountered in private life."

This is a reality that I, too, have regularly encountered from my nearly daily correspondence with the condemned. The result is a grotesque warping of Elizabeth Kubler-Ross's "Five Stages of Grief" into the whirlwind of fight, rage, grief, and isolation that Ms. Sullivan and Rev. Hood have depicted so powerfully in these pages. The result is an unmitigated abomination.

As Elie Wiesel famously said of capital punishment: "death should never be the answer in a civilized society." Indeed, as Ms. Sullivan and Rev. Hood have demonstrated beyond a shadow of a doubt: the death penalty condemns the society that enacts it infinitely more than any individual it condemns to die; indeed, it condemns us *all*.

And so, the thousands of members of the group I co-founded, L'chaim! Jews Against the Death Penalty stand with Ms. Sullivan and Rev. Hood as we ceaselessly chant: "L'chaim…to Life!"

Aza Chamavet Ahava ("Love is as strong as death.") - Song of Songs 8:6

Cantor Michael J. Zoosman, MSM

Board Certified Chaplain –Neshama: Association of Jewish Chaplains

Co-Founder: L'chaim! Jews Against the Death Penalty

Advisory Committee Member, Death Penalty Action